The Essential Guide to Self-Identit

A Book of Questions by Michael R.

Text Copyright © 2020 Michael R.B. Anderson

All rights reserved

Chief Editor Lexus Woodard

Cover photo by Tim Jonischkat, San Francisco 2014

Back Cover photo by Jimmy Armitage, China 2014

"A spontaneous moment of joy and innocence; of feeling the full power of life and all its endless journeys and dreams" - Jimmy Armitage 2020

Available online at www.amazon.com

All rights reserved. Non-commercial interests may reproduce portions of this book without the express written permission of the author, provided the text does not exceed 50 words. When reproducing text from this book, include the following credit line: "The Essential Guide to Self-Identity by Michael R.B. Anderson. Used by permission."

Commercial interests: No part of this publication may be reproduced in any form, stored in a retrieval system or transmitted in any form by any means – electronic, photocopy, recording, or otherwise – without prior written permission of the publisher, except as provided by the United States of America copyright law.

DEDICATION

Dedicated to all those who have an intensity about life, in what you do you demonstrate passion.

PREFACE

A Hero's Riddle

A Hero came along reverent and strong, challenged but belonged, developed in the world and time surely swirled, wisp and white, black in knight, a Hero's tale of discovery will delightfully ignite. Read as you wish, answer as you would like, you begin a Hero's tale of Self-Identity in life.

ACKNOWLEDGEMENTS

To Us

Family

The Education System

A Friend or Two

INTRODUCTION

To me, Self-Identity is absolutely necessary, essential, indispensable. To my readers, it may invoke thoughtfulness, discovery, adventure and wisdom. With this book, The Essential Guide to Self-Identity: A Book of Questions, take home with you and peek through the eyes of your inner self.

The Essential Guide to Self-Identity: A Book of Questions is a collection of questions I have held dearly since I was a young man. The questions from which you are about to read and answer as thoughtfully as you may, are of a simple origin, the minds of those who asked the question before me. Although our answers appear from a brain of our own, I surely appreciate their thoughtfulness entirely, "What a great question."

As we turn the pages of life, we encounter more and more questions from people that look at us for answers. The questions rarely change, although the answers vary far and in-between from this year to the next. I have thoughtfully outlined a pattern at which I seemingly arrived at my own sense of Identity, regardless the question. A secret I have chosen to share.

To the reader I share this secret, a secret you surely do not want to miss. I share this secret risk-free with you and assure you it enriches year after year. The pattern to obtain the secret is simple, it is within you.

May this book be a guide to its readers who keep coming back.

I Thank You.

TABLE OF CONTENTS

03
Preface

04
Acknowledgements

05
Introduction

07
Thoughtfulness

10
Discovery

20
Adventure

30
Wisdom

65
About The Author

THOUGHTFULNESS

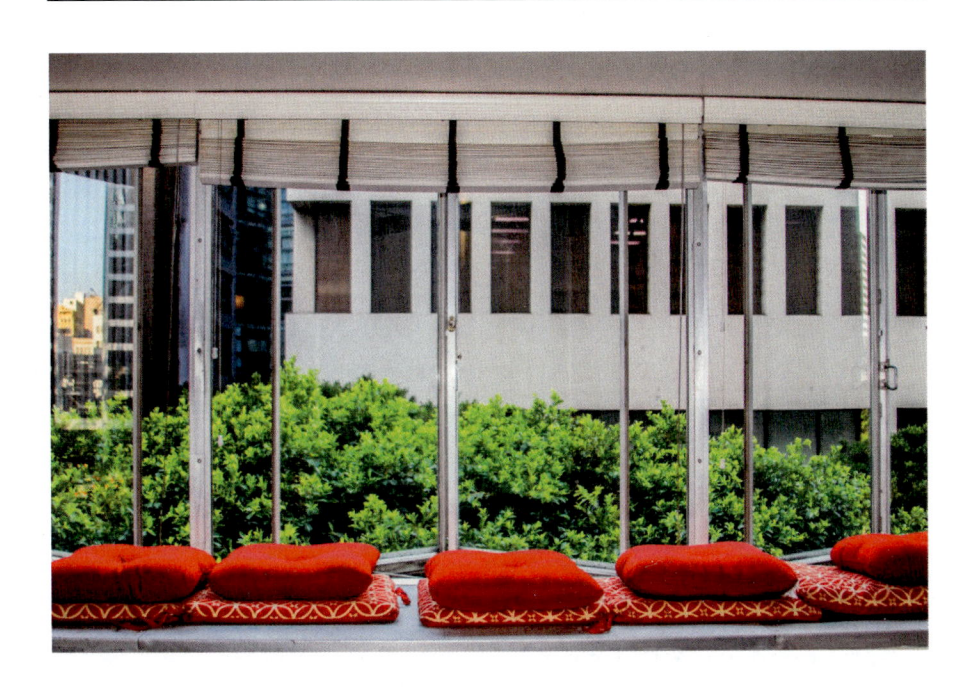

ARE YOU LIVING A MEANINGFUL LIFE?

WHAT ARE THE 5 MOST BEAUTIFUL THINGS IN THE WORLD?

WHAT OPPORTUNITIES ARE YOU LOOKING FOR?

WHEN IS THE NEXT TIME YOU WILL VISIT SOMEONE YOU LOVE?

WHAT IS THE FIRST THING YOU DO IN THE MORNING?

DISCOVERY

WHAT IS THE MOST VALUABLE THING YOU OWN?

IF YOU COULD TRADE PLACES WITH A CELEBRITY FOR A DAY, WHO WOULD YOU CHOOSE AND WHY?

WHAT HAVE YOU FOUND TO BE THE BEST WAY TO RELIEVE TENSION?

IF YOU COULD CHOOSE ONLY TWO MOVIES TO WATCH EVER AGAIN, WHAT WOULD THEY BE?

NAME THREE THINGS YOU WANTED AS A CHILD BUT NEVER GOT.

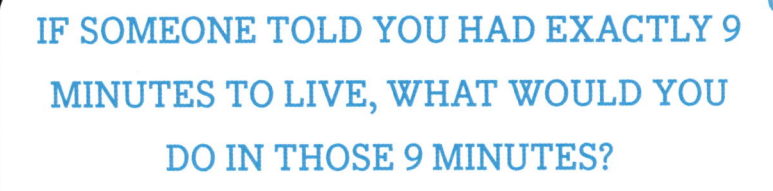

IF SOMEONE TOLD YOU HAD EXACTLY 9 MINUTES TO LIVE, WHAT WOULD YOU DO IN THOSE 9 MINUTES?

DESCRIBE YOUR DREAM HOUSE.

DO YOU BELIEVE PEOPLE ARE BASICALLY GOOD?

WHAT IS THE MOST EXPENSIVE ARTICLE OF CLOTHING YOU'VE EVER PURCHASED?

WHAT ARE YOUR WORST HABITS?

WHO IS THE PERSON YOU KNOW WITH THE PUREST SOUL?

DESCRIBE THE HAPPIEST DAY OF YOUR LIFE.

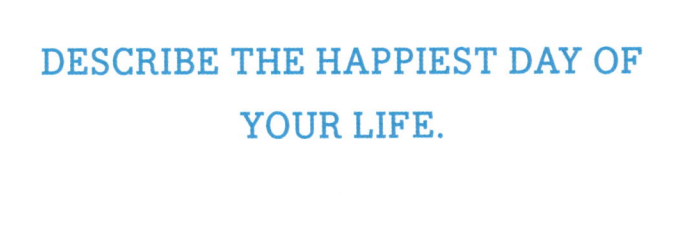

DESCRIBE THE SADDEST DAY OF YOUR LIFE.

WHAT IS THE OLDEST AGE YOU WOULD LIKE TO BE ALIVE?

WHAT WAS THE BEST YEAR OF YOUR LIFE?

WHO IS THE MOST SUCCESSFUL PERSON PERSONALLY KNOWN TO YOU?

WHO IS THE MOST OUTRAGEOUS PERSON PERSONALLY KNOWN TO YOU?

WHAT IS YOUR BIGGEST REGRET?

IF YOU COULD CHOOSE ONLY ONE MUSICAL ALBUM TO EVER LISTEN TO AGAIN, WHAT WOULD IT BE?

YOU CAN GO BACK IN TIME AND PREVENT A GREAT CATASTROPHE. WHICH ONE WOULD YOU PREVENT?

IF YOU WERE TO WRITE A LETTER TO YOUR FUTURE SELF WHAT WOULD THE LETTER SAY?

IF YOU WERE AT A FRIEND'S HOUSE FOR DINNER AND YOU FOUND THE FAMILY TO BE RUDE. WHAT WOULD YOU DO?

> IF YOU WERE ELECTED TO BE LEADER OF A FOREIGN COUNTRY TOMORROW, WHAT COUNTRY WOULD YOU WANT IT TO BE AND WOULD BE YOUR FIRST OFFICIAL ACT?

> WHAT IS YOUR ONE WISH FOR THE WORLD?

> YOU'VE JUST WON A COMPLETED COLLECTION OF MOVIES STARRING ONE ACTOR OR ACTRESS – WHICH ACTOR OR ACTRESS WOULD YOU PICK?

ADVENTURE

IS THERE SOMETHING YOU'VE DREAMED OF DOING FOR A LONG TIME? WHY HAVEN'T YOU DONE IT?

KNOWING YOU HAD A 50 PERCENT CHANCE OF WINNING AND WOULD BE PAID 10 TIMES THE AMOUNT OF YOUR BET IF YOU WON, WHAT FRACTION OF WHAT YOU NOW OWN WOULD YOU BE WILLING TO WAGER?

WHERE IS THE MOST BEAUTIFUL PLACE IN THE WORLD?

OF ALL THE PEOPLE CLOSE TO YOU, WHOSE DEATH WOULD YOU FIND MOST DISTURBING?

ONE HOT SUMMER AFTERNOON, WHILE WALKING THROUGH A PARKING LOT AT A LARGE SHOPPING CENTER, YOU NOTICE A DOG SUFFERING BADLY FROM THE HEAT INSIDE A LOCKED CAR. WHAT WOULD YOU DO?

IF YOU COULD GO BACK TO ANY DAY IN YOUR LIFE WHAT DAY WOULD IT BE AND WHY?

WHAT'S THE DUMBEST PURCHASE YOU'VE EVER MADE?

NAME THE MOST TERRIFYING MOMENT OF YOUR LIFE SO FAR.

IS RELIGION IMPORTANT TO YOU? DO YOU CONSIDER YOURSELF A RELIGIOUS PERSON? WOULD YOU EVER JUDGE SOMEONE ELSE FOR NOT HAVING THE SAME BELIEFS AS YOU?

THE MAJOR NEWSPAPER HEADLINES FOR TOMORROW WILL BE ABOUT YOU. WHAT WOULD YOU WANT THEM TO SAY?

NAME THREE EXPERIENCES INVOLVING A PET OR AN ANIMAL WHICH YOU WILL NEVER FORGET.

THROUGH A COMPUTER ERROR, YOU RECEIVE AN OVER PAYMENT ON YOUR PAYCHECK. DO YOU REPORT IT?

WHAT DO YOU LIKE BEST ABOUT YOUR LIFE? LEAST?

WHAT DO YOU THINK IS THE MOST IMPORTANT INVENTION OF THE LAST 100 YEARS?

WHAT WAS THE LAST DETAILED DREAM YOU REMEMBER?

WHAT HAS BEEN THE BIGGEST DISAPPOINTMENT IN YOUR LIFE?

WHO IS THE PERSON THAT YOU ONLY LET COME OUT WHEN NOBODY ELSE IS AROUND?

WHAT IS THE GREATEST ACCOMPLISHMENT OF YOUR LIFE? IS THERE ANYTHING YOU HOPE TO DO THAT IS EVEN BETTER?

WHAT IS THE MOST EMBARRASING THING TO EVER HAPPEN TO YOU?

WHAT IS THE MOST ROMANTIC PRESENT ANYONE HAS EVER GIVEN YOU?

WHAT IS THE MOST ROMANTIC SONG OR MUSIC YOU'VE EVER HEARD?

WHAT IS THE MOST USEFUL GIFT YOU'VE EVER BEEN GIVEN?

WHAT IS YOUR MOST TREASURED MEMORY?

WISDOM

WHO AM I?

WHAT AM I PASSIONATE ABOUT?

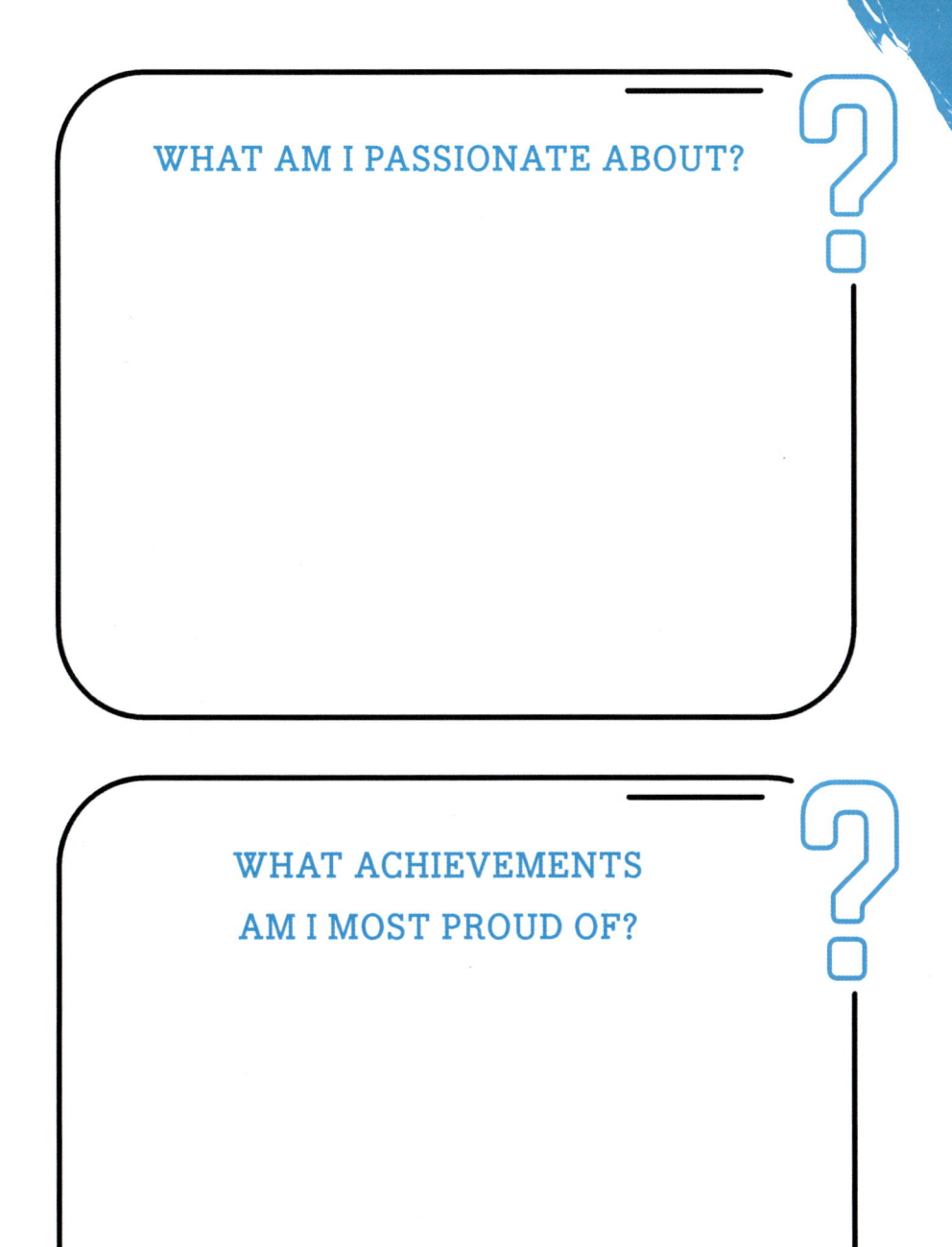

WHAT ACHIEVEMENTS AM I MOST PROUD OF?

WHAT AM I MOST GRATEFUL FOR IN LIFE?

WHAT ARE THE MOST IMPORTANT THINGS IN LIFE TO ME?

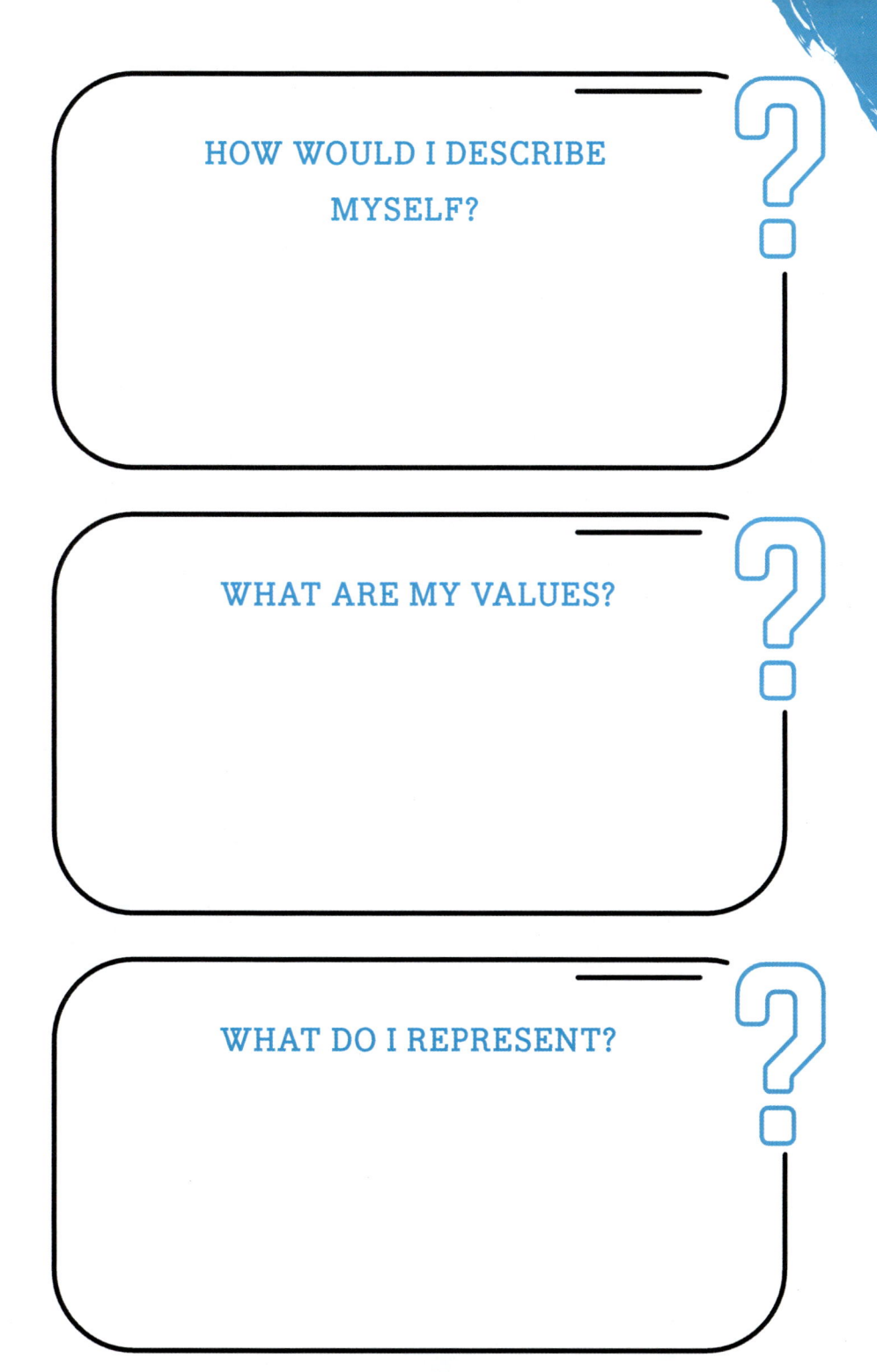

HOW WOULD I DESCRIBE MYSELF?

WHAT ARE MY VALUES?

WHAT DO I REPRESENT?

WHERE DO I ENJOY SPENDING MY TIME AND ENERGY?

DO I LOVE MYSELF?

HOW CAN I LOVE MYSELF MORE TODAY?

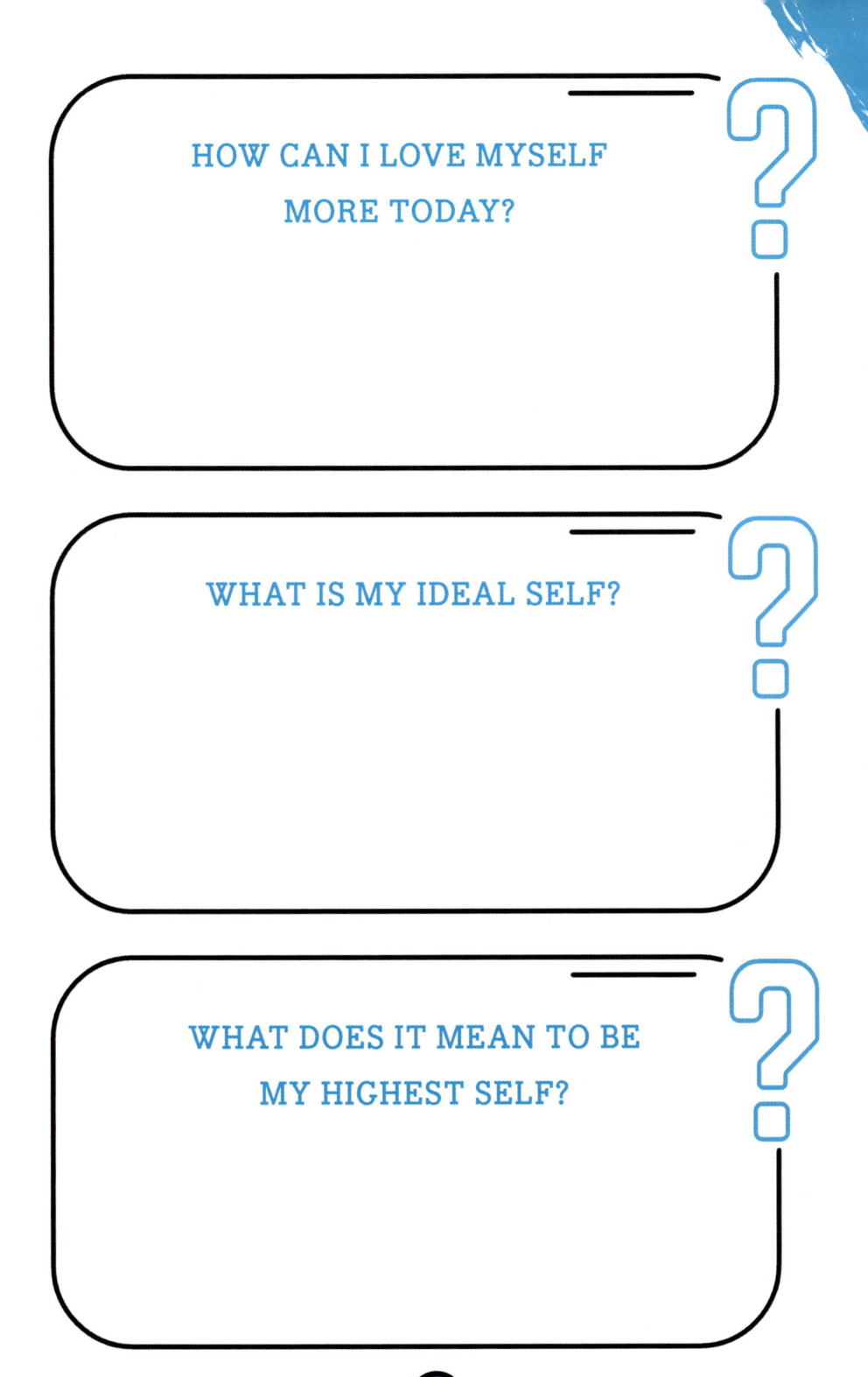

WHAT IS MY IDEAL SELF?

WHAT DOES IT MEAN TO BE MY HIGHEST SELF?

LOOK AT MY LIFE NOW. AM I
LIVING THE LIFE OF MY DREAMS?

IF I HAVE ONE YEAR LEFT TO
LIVE, WHAT WOULD I DO?

IF I HAVE ONE MONTH LEFT TO
LIVE, WHAT WOULD I DO?

IF I HAVE ONE WEEK LEFT TO LIVE, WHAT WOULD I DO?

IF I HAVE ONE DAY LEFT TO LIVE, WHAT WOULD I DO?

IF I HAVE AN HOUR LEFT TO LIVE, WHAT WOULD I DO?

IF I HAVE ONE-MINUTE LEFT TO LIVE, WHAT WOULD I DO?

WHAT WOULD I DO TODAY IF THERE WERE NO MORE TOMORROW?

WHAT ARE THE BIGGEST THINGS I'VE LEARNED IN LIFE TO DATE?

WHAT ADVICE WOULD I GIVE TO MYSELF 3 YEARS AGO?

IF I WERE MYSELF 1 YEAR FROM THE FUTURE, HOW WOULD I ADVISE ME?

IS THERE SOMETHING I'M STILL HOLDING ON TO? IS IT TIME TO LET IT GO?

WHAT AM I BUSY WITH TODAY? WILL THIS MATTER 1 YEAR FROM NOW? 3 YEARS? 5 YEARS?

WHAT OPPORTUNITIES AM I LOOKING FOR?

HOW CAN I CREATE THESE OPPORTUNITIES?

> WHAT ARE MY BIGGEST GOALS AND DREAMS?

> WHAT'S STOPPING ME FROM PURSUING THEM? WHY? HOW CAN I OVERCOME THEM?

> IF I AM TO DO SOMETHING FOR FREE FOR THE REST OF MY LIFE WHAT WOULD I WANT TO DO?

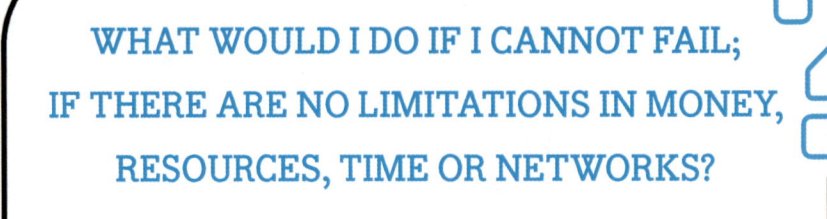

WHAT WOULD I DO IF I CANNOT FAIL; IF THERE ARE NO LIMITATIONS IN MONEY, RESOURCES, TIME OR NETWORKS?

WHAT DO I WANT TO ACHIEVE 1 YEAR FROM NOW? 3 YEARS? 5 YEARS? 10 YEARS?

HOW IMPORTANT ARE THESE GOALS TO ME?

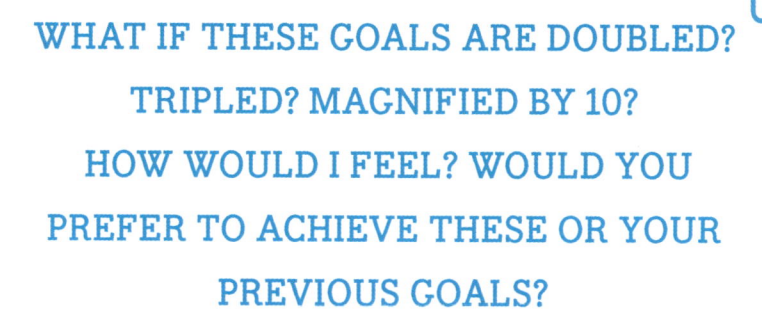

WHAT IF THESE GOALS ARE DOUBLED? TRIPLED? MAGNIFIED BY 10? HOW WOULD I FEEL? WOULD YOU PREFER TO ACHIEVE THESE OR YOUR PREVIOUS GOALS?

WHO ARE THE PEOPLE WHO HAVE ACHIEVED SIMILAR GOALS? WHAT CAN I LEARN FROM THEM?

AM I PUTTING ANY PARTS OF MY LIFE ON HOLD? WHY?

WHAT'S THE TOP PRIORITY IN MY LIFE RIGHT NOW? WHAT AM I DOING ABOUT IT?

IF I WERE TO DIE TOMORROW, WHAT WOULD BE MY BIGGEST REGRET?

HIGHLIGHT YOUR EXPERIENCES: WHAT ARE THE BIGGEST THINGS I HAVE LEARNED? HOW CAN I DO THIS BETTER THE NEXT TIME?

IF I HAD 1 MILLION DOLLARS, WHAT WOULD I DO WITH IT?

IF YOU COULD GIVE THE GIFT OF HAPPINESS TO THREE PEOPLE WHO WOULD IT BE?

WHAT IS MY IDEAL CAREER?

HOW CAN I START CREATING MY IDEAL CAREER STARTING TODAY?

WHAT IS MY IDEAL DIET?

WHAT DO I NEED TO DO TO ACHIEVE MY IDEAL DIET?

WHAT IS MY IDEAL HOME LIKE?

WHAT DO I NEED TO DO TO ACHIEVE MY IDEAL HOME?

WHAT IS MY IDEAL PHYSICAL LOOK?

WHAT DO I NEED TO ACHIEVE MY IDEAL PHYSICAL LOOK?

WHAT IS MY IDEAL LIFE?

WHAT CAN I DO TO START LIVING MY IDEAL LIFE?

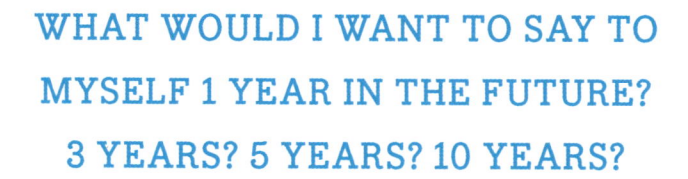

WHAT WOULD I WANT TO SAY TO MYSELF 1 YEAR IN THE FUTURE? 3 YEARS? 5 YEARS? 10 YEARS?

IF YOU CAN DO ONE THING WITHOUT SUFFERING THE CONSEQUENCES WHAT WOULD YOU DO?

IS HOME A FEELING OR A PHYSICAL PLACE FOR YOU?

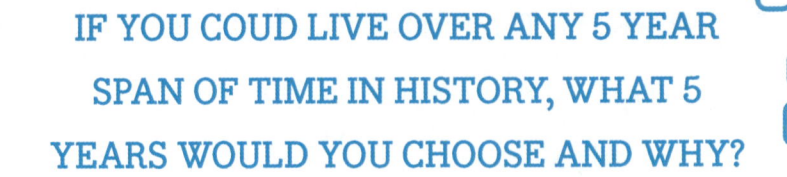

IF YOU COUD LIVE OVER ANY 5 YEAR SPAN OF TIME IN HISTORY, WHAT 5 YEARS WOULD YOU CHOOSE AND WHY?

WHAT DO I FEAR MOST IN LIFE?

IS THERE ANYTHING I AM RUNNING AWAY FROM?

AM I SETTLING FOR LESS THAN WHAT I AM WORTH? WHY?

WHAT IS MY INTERNAL DIALOGUE LIKE?

WHAT LIMITING BELIEFS AM I HOLDING ON TO?

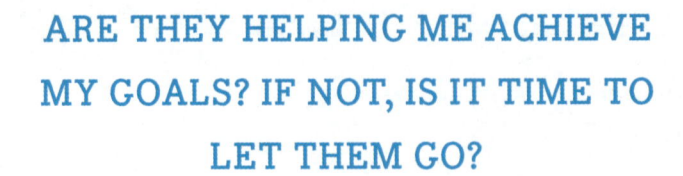

> **ARE THEY HELPING ME ACHIEVE MY GOALS? IF NOT, IS IT TIME TO LET THEM GO?**

> **WHAT EMPOWERING BELIEFS CAN I TAKE ON TO HELP ME ACHIEVE MY GOALS?**

> **WHAT BAD HABITS DO I WANT TO BREAK?**

WHAT GOOD HABITS DO I WANT TO CULTIVATE?

WHAT ARE THE BIGGEST ACTIONS I CAN TAKE NOW TO CREATE THE BIGGEST RESULTS?

WHERE AM I LIVING RIGHT NOW – THE PAST, FUTURE, OR PRESENT?

AM I LIVING MY LIFE TO THE FULLEST RIGHT NOW?

WHAT IS THE MEANING OF LIFE?

WHAT IS YOUR PURPOSE IN LIFE? WHY DO I EXIST? WHAT IS MY MISSION?

HOW CAN I MAKE MY LIFE MORE MEANINGFUL, STARTING TODAY?

WHAT DRIVES ME?

WHAT WERE THE TIMES I WAS MOST INSPIRED, MOST MOTIVATED, MOST CHARGED UP?

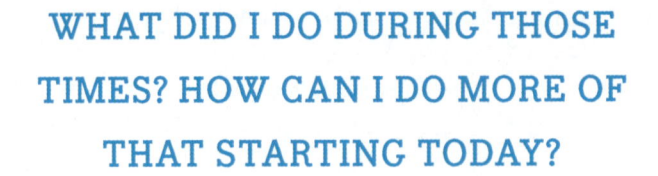

WHAT DID I DO DURING THOSE TIMES? HOW CAN I DO MORE OF THAT STARTING TODAY?

HOW CAN I CHANGE SOMEONE'S LIFE FOR THE BETTER TODAY?

WHO ARE THE 5 PEOPLE I SPEND THE MOST TIME WITH?

ARE THESE PEOPLE ENABLING ME OR HOLDING ME BACK?

WHAT QUALITIES DO I WANT TO EMBODY? WHERE CAN I MEET PEOPLE WHO EMBODY THESE QUALITIES?

WHO INSPIRES ME THE MOST?

HOW CAN I BE LIKE THEM?

WHAT IS MY IDEAL LIFE PARTNER LIKE?

WHERE CAN I MEET HIM/HER?

- HOW CAN I GET TO KNOW HIM/HER?

- AM I AFRAID OF LETTING OTHERS GET CLOSE TO ME? WHY?

- WHO IS/ARE THE MOST IMPORTANT PERSON(S) TO ME IN THE WORLD?

- AM I GIVING THEM THE ATTENTION I WANT TO GIVE?

- HOW CAN I SPEND MORE TIME WITH THEM STARTING TODAY?

- WHAT KIND OF PERSON DO I ENJOY SPENDING TIME WITH?

> HOW CAN I BE THIS PERSON TO OTHERS?

> WHO DO I WANT TO BE LIKE IN 1 YEAR? 3 YEARS? 5 YEARS? 10 YEARS?

> WHAT IS MY FAVORITE QUESTION FROM THIS BOOK?

WHO ARE THE 5 PEOPLE I AM GOING TO SHARE THIS BOOK WITH?

WRITE YOUR OWN QUESTION

WRITE YOUR OWN QUESTION.

WRITE YOUR OWN QUESTION.

WRITE YOUR OWN QUESTION.

WRITE YOUR OWN QUESTION.

WHAT DO I WANT TO BE REMEMBERED AS?

ABOUT THE AUTHOR

Mr. Michael R.B. Anderson a man of greater character and sound judgment.

Michael personified what it means to be well-rounded. Michael's outlook on life seemingly progressive, thought provoking and well received by those with strong moral values centered on family, philanthropy, community, fairness, environment, humanity, decency and culture.

Michael's legacy

A meaningful life wondering the world time and time again.

Have a firm handshake.

Look people in the eye.

Sing in the shower.

Own a great sound system.

If in a fight, hit first and hit hard.

Keep secrets.

Never give up on anybody.
Miracles happen every day.

Always accept an
outstretched hand. Be brave.

Even if you're not, pretend to be.
No one can tell the difference.

Whistle.

Avoid sarcastic remarks.

Choose your life's partner carefully.
From this one decision will come 90 per cent of all your happiness or misery.

Make it a habit to do nice things for people who will never find out.

Lend only those books
you never care to see again.

Never deprive someone of hope;
it might be all that they have.

When playing games with children,
let them win.

Give people a second chance,
but not a third.

Be romantic.

Become the most positive and
enthusiastic person you know.

Loosen up. Relax. Except for rare
life-and-death matters, nothing is as
important as it first seems.

Don't allow the phone to interrupt important moments.
It's there for our convenience, not the caller's.

Be a good loser.

Be a good winner.

Think twice before burdening a friend with a secret.

When someone hugs you, let them be the first to let go.

Be modest. A lot was accomplished before you were born.

Keep it simple.

Beware of the person who has nothing to lose.

Don't burn bridges. You'll be surprised how many times you have to cross the same river.

Live your life so that your epitaph could read, No Regrets

Be bold and courageous. When you look back on life, you'll regret the things you didn't do more than the ones you did.

Never waste an opportunity to tell someone you love them.

Remember no one makes it alone. Have a grateful heart and be quick to acknowledge those who helped you.

Take charge of your attitude. Don't let someone else choose it for you.

Visit friends and relatives when they are in the hospital; you need only stay a few minutes.

Begin each day with some of your favorite music.

Once in a while, take the scenic route.

Send a lot of Valentine cards. Sign them, 'Someone who thinks you're terrific.'

Answer the phone with enthusiasm and energy in your voice.

Keep a note pad and pencil on your bedside table. Million-dollar ideas sometimes strike at 3 a.m.

Show respect for everyone who works for a living, regardless of how trivial their job.

Send your loved one's flowers. Think of a reason later.

Make someone's day by playing the toll for the person in the car behind you.

Become someone's hero.

Marry only for love.